Job Degenaar

Ich bin
I am

Inhalt
Inhoud

1

*

2

Eilanden
Inseln

3
Content of

I am

1

Wat avond met een haven doet

Gewichtloos glinsterwater
de havenlichten wiegen
vissersboten liggen
in blauw verankerd

Een man, roerloze reiger
zit in brons gegoten
in z'n hand een schepnet
waaruit geolied daglicht lekt

hij beweegt, haalt uit
een plons, maar niets
dan zijn silhouet met net
en het fronsen van de rivier

Zo leeg is het nu geworden
dat iemand sterren strooit
en het intiem rumoer me wenkt
dat uit verre bars bij vlagen aanwaait

Was Abend mit einem Hafen tut

Gewichtloses Flimmerwasser
die Hafenlichter wiegen sich
Fischerboote liegen
in Blau verankert

Ein Mann, ruderloser Reiher
sitzt in Bronze gegossen
in seiner Hand ein Käscher
woraus gut geöltes Tageslicht tropft

Er regt sich, schlägt zu
ein Klatsch, aber nichts
als sein Schattenriß mit Netz
und das Kräuseln, vom Fluß

So leer ist es jetzt geworden
daß jemand Sterne streut
und das intime Tosen mir winkt
aus fernen Bars bei wehenden Fahnen

Augustus, halverwege

Over het land verspreidt zich
een zweem van herfst: dun
waas boven de sloten, de stille
voltooiing van zoete vruchten
en een naderend gevoel van
verlorenheid dat al sluimert
in de mooiste liefdesnachten

August, auf halbem Weg

Über dem Land verbreitet sich
ein Schimmern von Herbst: dünn
über den Schlössern, die stille
Ausreifung der süßen Früchte
und ein sich näherndes Gefühl von
Verlorenheit das schon schlummert
in den schönsten Liebesnächten

Lentemerel in Sarajevo

Na het uitgedunde licht
de geweren, het verdriet
eindelijk de lentemerel

De lange winter heeft men zich
gekeerd tegen dood en verval
in kleine vertrekken afgezonderd
hout en broden aangedragen
zich verhit en getest aan elkaar

tijd werd als een lastdier voortgejaagd
door de arena van een karig leven
toekomst bezworen met kalenders

van verlatenheid heelde hartzeer
groeide op dunne wanden eelt
slibden we koel en weerbarstig dicht

Kom, lente, als een eerste morgen
omnevel heuvels, rivieren, dorpen
dat we langzaam weerloos worden

als bunkers belaagd door vrede

Frühjahrsamsel in Sarajevo

Nach den eisigen Nächten
die gewesen, dem Verdruß
endlich die Frühjahrsamsel

gedreht gegen Tod und Verfall
in kleinen Abschieden abgesondert
Holz und Brote herbeigetragen
sich erhitzt und aneinander getestet

Zeit wird als ein Lastesel gejagt
durch die Arena eines dürftigen Lebens
Zukunft beschworen mit Kalendern

von Verlassensein völligem Herzschmerz
wuchs auf dünnen Wänden Hornhaut
schlämmen wir kühl und widerborstig dicht

Komm, Frühling, als ein erster Morgen
umnebelte Hügel, Flüsse, Dörfer
daß wir langsam wehrlos werden

als Bunker belagert durch Frieden

ONDER een maïsgele sombrero
met kleine implosies soms onder
de dunne voering van m'n huid
sta ik, vluchteling, zanger
aan de rand van een millennium
met een gitaar om m'n nek
in een Mexicaans eethuis
diep in Holland
Als ik zing, zingt m'n land
als ik zwijg, rouwt het

en Juanita zomert de tafels langs
de airco beweegt haar bloesje
er is bier en de Balkan is ver
en ach, wie hoort
dat ik Bosniër ben
wie decodeert m'n zonnige fratsen
dan wie mij volgden: vrouw en kind
aan de bar, stille meeuwen
vervreemd van hun kust, achter
een schip aan, ver overzee

UNTER einem maisgelben Sombrero
mit kleinen Implosionen manchmal unter
der dünnen Auskleidung meiner Haut
stehe ich, Flüchtling, Sänger
am Rande des Jahrtausends
mit einer Gitarre um meinen Hals
in einem Mexiko-Speisehaus
tief in Holland.
Wenn ich singe singt mein Land
wenn ich schweige trauert es

und Juanita sommert die Tische entlang
die Klimaanlage läßt ihre Bluse wehen
da ist Bier und der Balkan ist fern
und ach, wer hört
daß ich Bosnier bin
wer entschlüsselt meine sonnigen Fratzen
dann wer mir folgte: Frau und Kind
an der Bar, stille Möwen
in der Ferne weg von ihrer Küste, hinter
einem Schiff her, weit über die See

De vrouw die in mij woont

De vrouw die in mij woont
kijkt uit het raam van een stil huis
en laaft zich aan de fado, de weemoed
van de cello, het vuur van de gitaar
de waaierende zang

minstens één vergeefse liefde
kent ze, een val die haar deed
wankelen en misschien
een vijand in haar vlees

mooier is ze dan haar leven
zachter haar strelen dan haar handen
dieper haar kussen dan haar mond

De vrouw die in mij woont
werd onvermijdelijk poëzie

Die Frau die in mir wohnt

Die Frau die in mir wohnt
schaut aus dem Fenster eines stillen Hauses
und labt sich am Fado, der Wehmut
des Cellos, dem Feuer der Gitarre
der flatternde Gesang

mindestens eine vergebliche Liebe
kennt sie, ein Fall der sie ließ
wanken und vielleicht
ein Feind in ihrem Fleisch

schöner ist sie als ihr Leben
zärtlicher ihr Streicheln als ihre Hände
tiefer ihr Küssen als ihr Mund

Die Frau die in mir wohnt
wird unvermeidlich Poesie

Brocken Spectre

Nichts ist andauernder als der Wechsel
nichts beständiger als der Tod

Ludwig Börne (1825)

Twee eeuwen later alsnog
de Spitz bestegen, in het spoor
van Goethe, Hoffmann, Heine

Ook ik zag achter dennen glippen
het volkje dat 's nachts broden steelt
en room likt van de melk

en over mij vloog een kattenschim
die een heks op bezem werd
op weg naar het Walpurgisfest

Bijna boven, op het stomp plateau
verwaterde de morgenzon terwijl
de schaduw van m'n hoofd maar zwol

en, zwaar van het aureool, tegen
een mistbank leunde: droom die telkens
me bezoekt, het eind nabij zie ik

die laat-romantische kop van mij
potsierlijk uitvergroot
en daarna krimpen tot het bot

16

Bandbreiten Brocken

Nichts ist andauernder als der Wechsel
nichts beständiger als der Tod

Börne 1825

Zwei Jahrhunderte später noch
den Spitz bestiegen in der Spur
von Goethe, Hoffmann, Heine

Und ... ja, auch ich sah hinter Tannen rutschen
das Völklein das des Nachts die Brote stiehlt
und den Rahm wegleckt von der Milch

und über mich hinweg flog da ein Katzenschattenbild
das zu einer Hexe auf dem Besen wird
auf dem Weg zum Walpurgisnachtfest

Beinahe obenauf, auf der stumpfigen Hochebene
verwässerte die Morgensonne sich zugleich
und der Schatten meines Hauptes blähte

und, schwer von diesem Glorienschein, gegen
eine Nebelbank gelehnt, Traum der immer wieder
mich besucht, das Ende nahe bei sehe ich

das spätromantische Kopfstück von mir
possierlich herausvergrößert
und danach schrumpfen bis zum Knochen

Achtung: Hochspannung!

Langs zandwarme oevers glijden we
en koeien, grazend door de nevel, dammen
waar aalscholvers hun veren strekken
de glooiingen met druivenstokken
het veer dat drie auto's overzet
de vuilnisdienst met *Abfall ist unser Fall*

en gaan voorbij aan de diep
gedolven waarheid van een kolenschip
en rijnaken met duistere namen als
Anaconda, Diablo, Hercules IV: decors
schuivend door je netvlies, glinsters
opduwend vanonder hun bodems

En daar, op weg naar sluizen die ons hoger
en hoger tillen, ligt het dan: Bella Italia
aan de Moezel, onder hoogspanningskabels
die zich als feestslingers spreiden over heuvels
zacht snorrend naar de smeltende chocola
van hooggelegen Fachbauhuizen

stroomstoten gevend aan een snel blekend
landschap dat minder schokt dan op het dek
het blauw geknetter van een val
met daaronder een hoopje vlinders:
spel voor de wind
stof voor een nieuwe dag

Achtung Hochspannung!

Entlang warmsandigen Ufern gleiten wir
und Kühe, grasend durch den Nebel, Dämme
wo Kormorane ihre Federn strecken
das Gefälle mit Traubenstöcken
die Fähre die drei Autos herüberbringt
den Müllwagen von *Abfall ist unser Fall*

und gehen vorbei an der tiefen
ausgegrabenen Wahrheit von einem Kohlenschiff
und Rheinkähne mit düsteren Namen wie
Anaconda, Diabolo, Hercules IV: Hintergrundkulissen
schieben sich über deine Netzhaut, Glitzer
taucht auf aus ihren Böden

Und dort, auf dem Weg zu Schleusen die uns höher
und höher heben liegt es da: Bella Italia
an der Mosel, unter Hochspannungskabeln
die sich als Luftschlangen über Hügel winden
leicht surrend zum schmilzenden Schoko
von hochgelegenen Fachwerkhäusern

Stromstöße austeilend an eine schnell ausbleichende
Landschaft, aber weniger elektrisierend
als auf der Decke das blaue Geprassel
eines Falles mit darunter einem Haufen
Schmetterlingen: Spiel für den Wind
Staub für einen neuen Tag

2

Domino Day

Hoe haar oogopslag
die oude eik

de eik de wei
de wei de sloot

de sloot de lucht
de lucht m'n lijf

nog net
in lichterlaaie zet

Dominotag

Wie ihr Augenaufschlag
die alte Eiche

die Eiche die Weide
die Weide der Abschlußgraben

der Graben die Luft
die Luft mein Leib

gerade noch
ins Lichterlohe setzt

Métropolitain

Kruispunt van wie komt en gaat
zwijgende stroom in de tijd
de op- en afgeleefden
met liefde of dood in hun ogen

De verliezers herschikken zich
in de smalle straten met de smalle
huizen, de smalle kaders
waarin ze elkaar verdringen

om de ondraaglijk
wijde lucht daarboven

Metropole

Kreuzpunkt derer die kommen und gehen
schweigender Strom in der Zeit
die Auf und Ab Gelebten
mit Liebe und Tod im Auge

Die Verlierer gruppieren sich neu
in schmalen Strassen mit schmalen
Häusern, die schmalen Rahmen
worin sie sich ineinander verheddern

für die unerträglich
weite Luft da oben

LANG na het paradijs
dook in het tropendonker
een nachtvlinder op
een lichte flikkering
die alle nachten
mij zou bezoeken

eenzaam van verrukking
volgde ik haar

Avond in een ander leven
de buitenwijken staren
binnen slaat stilte
haar ultieme slag

ik speur de lege hemel af

LANG nach dem Paradies
tauchte im Tropendunkel
ein Nachtfalter auf
ein leichtes Flittern
der all die Nächte
mich besuchen sollte

einsam durch Entrückung
folgte ich diesem

Abend in einem anderen Leben
die Außenbezirke starren
innen schlägt Stille
ihren letztendlichen Schlag

ich spüre den leeren Himmel ab

Rivieroever in grijs

Misschien zijn meisjes uit Japan hier nodig
drie in lila, roze, wit, onder een parasol van riet
op smalle voeten over het bleke zand

de wind stak op, het water ruiste
en wolken buitelden door het blauw
of ze heel de aarde nog over moesten

en waar in de verte de rivier verdroomt
stroomde het goud van boeddha
over de uitgewoonde harten

Flußufer in Grau

Vielleicht sind junge Frauen aus Japan hier vonnöten
drei in Lila, rosafarben, Weiß unter einem
                        Sonnenschirm von Stroh
auf schmalen Füssen über bleichen Sand

der Wind frischte auf, das Wasser rauschte
und Wolken beutelten sich durchs Blau
alsob sie noch ganz über die Erde mußten

und wo in der Ferne der Fluß sich verträumt
strömte das Gold des Buddha
über die ausgewohnten Herzen

Bericht voor reizigers naar het zuiden

Met gewapend glas om u heen en
voor het dagelijks sterven wat passie
die uw leven stut, komt u ver als u
die koppelt aan geduld en proviand

achter de bergen verstuiven de wolken
doemen andere decors op, ook u bent
alleen decor, voorbij het verkeersgedruis
ligt onder de maan uw droomzee

Eerst zult u, onhandige duif, klapwieken
in uw te uitgedijd heelal en hinder ondervinden
van werkzaamheden in uw ziel omtrent verlies
in allerlei soorten zoals het doven van heimwee

idolen die van hun stuk vielen en een dierbare
die ophield te bestaan omdat iets hem of haar
plotseling opeiste: dan is er geen troost
dan wat regels uit een duurzaam boek

Snij het geluk dat in u sluimert aan
en deel het met uw naasten, kerf
levenstekens in levenstekens, ontkurk
een roes die uw bestaan verruimt

en zie: de hevig
gewenste nacht, zacht
sterren wiegend
in uw hangmat

Bericht für Reisende in den Süden

Panzerglas um euch herum
für das tägliche Sterben etwas Leidenschaft
die euer Leben stützt, kommt ihr weit wenn ihr
die koppelt an Geduld und Proviant

hinter den Bergen zerschellen die Wolken
erscheinen andere Verzierungen, auch ihr seid
allein Dekor, vorbei das Verkehrsgebrause
liegt unter dem Mond euer Traumozean

Zuerst sollt ihr, tapsige Taube, flattern
in eurem übergroßen Weltall und Ungemach fühlen
von Aktivitäten eurer Seele sich beziehend auf Verlust
aller Arten so wie das Betäuben des Heimwehs
-
Idole die zustück fielen und ein Teurer
der aufhörte zu sein weil etwas ihn oder sie
plötzlich forderte: dann ist da kein Trost
als Zeilen aus einem wertvollen Buch

öffnet das Glück schlummernd in dir
und teilt es mit mit eueren Nächsten, schnitze
Lebenszeichen in Lebenszeichen, entkorke
einen Rausch der euer Sein erweitert

und siehe: die heftig
gewünschte Nacht, sanft
Sterne wiegend
in euerer Hängematte

Ich bin

Zwaar van bloesem buigt vanavond
de oude appelboom

en zij daar, satijnen engel
althans vanuit m'n auto

detonerend in de leegte
haalt haar wasgoed van de lijn

Ook op de radio komt ze door
'von Kopf bis Fuß auf Liebe eingestellt'

Even scheurt de grond -
Berlin dreißiger Jahre

und überall
Wege zum Glück -

Het huis herzien, de boom geveld
de polder bijna ingevuld

de weg is recht, m'n leven krom
ik kijk nog altijd even om

Ich bin

Schwer von Blüten beugt sich heute abend
der alte Apfelbaum

und sie da, Engel von Satin
zumindest aus meinem Auto

fehl am Platz in die Leere
holt ihre Wäsche von der Leine

Auch im Radio kommt sie durch
von Kopf bis Fuß auf Liebe eingestellt

Gerade tut sich der Boden auf
Berlin 30er-Jahre

und überall
Wege zum Glück -

Das Haus wiedergesehen, der Baum gefällt
die Polderwelt ist fast gefüllt

der Weg ist gerade mein Leben krumm
ich sehe mich immer noch einmal um

Vluchtgegevens

Een stewardess speelt noodtoneel
de avondster zweeft in het raam
de maan ligt op haar rug

tijd is eindelijk stilgezet
we hangen in de lucht
Tot beneden, roodbruin, land daagt

dat trillend op zijn fundamenten
ons aanzuigt als een magneet
een stofwolk rolt een zandpad over

De schaduw van het vliegtuig
koerst af op een minaret
een flat en de lichte

onrust die ontstaat
als iets de grond raakt
van de dingen

Flugtatsachen

Eine Stewardess spielt Nottheater
der Abendstern schwebt im Fenster
der Mond liegt auf dem Rücken

Zeit ist letztendlich festgeschraubt
wir hängen in der Luft
Bis unten, rotbraun, Land hellt auf

das zitternd auf seine Fundamente
uns zieht wie ein Magnet
eine Staubwolke überrollt den Pfad im Sand

Der Schatten von einem Flugzeug
Kurs auf ein Minarett
eine kleine Wohnung und die leichte

Unruh' die entsteht
wenn etwas den Boden berührt
der Dinge

Familieberaad aan de rivier

In de middaghitte blijven zitten
onder een eeuwdikke kastanje
bij café de Overzet, waar een smalle
Maas verkoeling aanvoert

de glijbaan slijt een kinderjurk, de schommel
wil maar niet vergaan, en wij, familie, voor
even verenigd, praten dat het een drukte is
over de vluchtigheid van het leven

Later zou het stiller worden, ontweken
de kippen ons minder, zagen we in de verte
hoe nog de trekpont fietsers overzette
en de zon zich languit over het water legde

Dit was onze wereld niet
dit waren wij

Familienberaten am Fluß

In der Mittagshitze sitzen bleiben
unter jahrhundertdickem Kastanienbaum
beim Café an der Fähre wo eine schmale
Maas Abkühlung schickt

die Rutsche zerschlitzt ein Kinderkleid, die Schaukel
will einfach nicht vergehen, und wir, Familie, für
jetzt vereinigt, sprechen bis zum Hochdruck
über die Flüchtigkeit des Lebens

Später sollte es stiller werden, entweichen
die Hühner uns fast nicht mehr, sahen wir in der Ferne
wie noch die Handfähre die Fahrradfahrer rüberbrachte
die Sonne sich lang über das Wasser legte

Dies war nicht unsere Welt
dies waren wir

Sneeuw

Sneeuw is een sprookje
een maagdelijke hoer

met haar smetteloze schijn
is zij de koningin van het oppervlak

Maar ze bedriegt je onderlangs
als ze in de middag murmelend

opbrandt en er door haar huid
weer vragen schemeren

Schnee

Schnee ist ein Märchen
jungfräuliche Hure

mit seinem schmutzlosen Schein
ist er König der Oberfläche

Aber er bedroht dich von unten her
als er in den Mittag murmelt

entbrannt und da durch die Haut
wieder Fragen schimmern

Thuiskomst

Hartgrondig tegen de dood geleefd
tot iets onverwacht je spiegelt
een gedicht bijvoorbeeld, zo

broos dat je nooit dacht
dat het bestond
Dat zich wringt

uit al je poriën, opstaat
van het papier en je
aankijkt als een ree

Dat is nog eens thuiskomen:
zien wie je bent
op dit moment

Nachhausekommen

Von ganzem Herzen gegen den Tod gelebt
bis etwas unerwartetes dich spiegelt
ein Gedicht zum Beispiel, so

zerbrechlich daß du nie dachtest
daß es da
das sich auswringt

aus allen Poren heraus, aufsteht
aus dem Papier und dich
anschaut wie ein Reh

Das ist nach Hause kommen:
zu sehen wer du bist
in diesem Augenblick

De kunst van het dichten

Ik geloof in het paardenbloempluisje
waaraan je je vertilt als je het vangen wil

en dat je in een zucht wegblaast
zodra het je verveelt

Dat zoveel ruimte aan je laat
dat het er bijna niet is als het er is

maar dat met fijne weerhaakjes
toch de aarde aan zich bindt

Die Kunst des Dichtens

Ich glaube an das Löwenzahnpropellerlein
woran du dich verhebst beim Fangen

das du mit einem Zug wegbläst
sobald es dir Langeweile bringt

Das so viel Platz an dir läßt
das beinahe nicht ist wenn es da

aber das mit feinen Widerhäkchen
doch die Erde an sich bindet

Eilanden
Inseln

DE boot naar Ameland is leeg
de golven slaan tegen de reling
asbakken rinkelen met de motoren mee

we zitten verloren in onszelf, zien
de kade naderen, hoe de lampen zwiepen
en een oude regen over de huizen trekt

Nu de wind elke gedachte belaagt
murmelt een mondharmonica
dat het meisje mooi is

en de eenzame lach
van een vrouw naar een man
pulseert door de salon

DAS Boot nach Ameland ist leer
die Wellen schlagen gegen die Reling
Aschenbecher klinkern mit den Motoren mit

Wir sitzen in uns selbst verloren, sehen
den Kai sich nähern, wie die Lampen schwenken
und ein alter Regen über die Häuser zieht

Jetzt da der Wind jeden Gedanken belagert
murmelt eine Mundharmonika
daß das Mädchen wunderschön

und das einsame Lachen
einer Frau zu einem Mann
pulsierend durch den Salon

Schiermonnikoog

Hier nu zindert het licht niet meer
de stoelen op het strandterras
hurken als oudgedienden bij elkaar

het is gebeurd dus tussen ons
en alles van toen is zilver:
dit eiland, de zee, de vogels

'Passing ships have come and gone
just you and me to lean upon'
Maar de meeuwen riepen dat het tijd was

Wat bleef is een bewogen foto
je hennahaar verwaaid aan een zee
die allerinnemendst liegt

Schiermonnikoog

Hier jetzt flirrt das Licht nicht mehr
die Stühle auf der Strandterasse
hocken als Altgediente beieinander

es ist passiert also zwischen uns
und alles aus Gestern ist Silber:
dieses Eiland, die See, die Vögel

Passing ships have come and gone
just you and me to lean upon
Aber die Möwen riefen daß es Zeit

Was blieb ist ein verwischtes Foto
dein Hennahaar verweht an eine See
die alle einnehmend hier liegt

I am
Ich bin

What night does to a harbour

Weightless glinting water
the harbour lights sway
fisher boats lie
anchored in blue

A man, unstirring heron
sits cast in bronze
in his hand a dip-net
that leaks oiled daylight

he stirs, strikes hard
a splash, but nothing
other than his silhouette and net
and the river's wrinkles

So empty it has now become
that someone sprinkles stars
and the intimate clamour calls to me
that blows in gusts from bars afar

August, halfway

Over the land spreads
a shadow of fall: thin
veil over the ditches, the silent
fulfilling of sweet fruit
in a creeping feeling
of forlornness already slumbering
in the most splendid nights of love

Spring blackbird in Sarajevo

After the thinned out light
the rifles, the sorrow
finally the spring blackbird

Along long winter one has
turned against death and decay
in small chambers isolated
wood and bread carried in
getting hot and tested to each other

time was chased like a beast of burden
through the arena of a sparse life
the future allayed with calendars

of having been left the heart healed
on these walls grew calluses
cool and contrary we got clogged

Come spring, as a first morn
mist up hills, rivers, villages
so that slowly we will be defenceless

as bunkers besieged by peace

UNDER a corn yellow sombrero
with some small implosions under
the thin lining of my skin
I fugitive, singer stand
at the edge of a millennium
with a guitar strapped to my neck
in a Mexican eatery
deep in Holland
When I sing, sings my country
when I keep still, it mourns

and Juanita summers along the tables
the air conditioning moves her blouse
there is beer and the Balkans are far away
and well, who hears
that I am from Bosnia
who decodes my sunny pranks
but who followed me: wife and child
at the bar, silent seagulls
estranged from their coast, behind
a ship, far over sea

The woman who lives within me

The woman who lives within me
looks out of the window of a quiet house
and laps up the fado, the melancholy
of the cello, the fire of the guitar
the unfolding vocal

at least one fruitless love
she knows, a fall that made her
stagger and perhaps
an enemy in her flesh

more beautiful she is than her life
softer her caresses than her hands
deeper her kisses than her mouth

The woman who lives within me
unavoidably became poetry

Brocken Spectre

Nothing is more lasting but change
Nothing more permanent than death

Ludwig Börne (1825)

Two centuries later after all
climbed the Peak, on the trail
of Goethe, Hoffmann, Heine

Also I saw slip away behind firs
the wee folks who at night steal the bread
lick the cream off the milk

and over me flew a cat-shade
turning into a witch on broom
on her way to the Walpurgis Night

Almost there on the blunt plateau
the morning sun watered down while
the shadow of my head kept swelling

and heavy with halo, leaned
against a bank of fog: dream revisiting
me every time, the end near I see

that late-romantic head of mine
ridiculously aggrandized
and then shrinking to bare bone

Achtung Hochspannung! - Attention High Voltage!

Along sand-warm shores we glide
and cows, grazing through mist, dams
where cormorants stretch their feathers
the slopes with grape-palings
the ferry ferried three cars
the garbage service with *Abfall ist unser Fall -*
Trash is our cash
and pass the deeply
delved truth of a coal boat
and Rhine barges with dark names as
Anaconda, Diablo, Hercules IV: scenery
sliding by your retina, bringing up
sparkles from beneath their bottoms

And there, on our way to lock which higher
and higher carry us, there it lies: Bella Italia
on the Moselle, under high voltage cables
spreading themselves as garlands over hills
softly zooming to the melting chocolate
of high harbored fachwerk houses

giving jolts of currents to a fast paling
landscape which moves less than on the deck
the blue thundering of a fall
under it a bunch of butterflies:
play for the wind
dust for a new day

Domino Day

How her glance
that old oak

the oak the meadow
the meadow the ditch

the ditch the air
the air my body

just still
lights my fire

Metropolitan

Crossroads of who comes and goes
silent stream of time
the lived up and down
with love or death in their eyes

The losers regroup
in the narrow streets with the narrow
houses, the narrow frames
in which they crowd each other

for the unbearably
wide sky above

LONG after paradise
surfaced in tropical dark
a night-butterfly
a light glimmer
which every night
would visit me

lonesome with bliss
I followed her

Evening in a different life
suburbia stares
inside silence deals
its ultimate blow

I scan the empty sky

Riverbank in grey

Maybe girls from Japan are needed here
three in lilac, pink, white, under a parasol of reed
on narrow feet over pale sand

the wind rose, the water rustled
and clouds tumbled through the blue
as if they still had the whole earth to cross

and where in the distance the river dreams away
streamed the gold of Buddha
over the run down hearts

Message for travellers to the south

With reinforced glass around you and
for the daily dying some passion
shoring up your life, you'll get far if you
match it with patience and provisions

behind the mountains the clouds dissipate
different decors appear, you too are
but decor, past the traffic noise
lies under the moon your sea of dreams

First you will, clumsy dove, flap your wings
in your too widened universe and be hampered
by workings in your soul dealing with loss
of all kinds, like the homesickness to be dowsed

idols falling from their pedestal and a loved one
who stopped existing because something suddenly
claimed him or her: then there is no consolation
but a few lines in a time tested book

Cut up the happiness slumbering in you
and share it with your close ones, carve
signs of life in signs of life, uncork
a high enhancing your existence

and see: the fiercely
wished for night, quietly
cradling the stars
in your hammock

Ich bin, I am

Blossom heavy bows tonight
the old apple tree

and she there, satin angel
at least from my car

incongruent in the emptiness
takes the laundry off the line

Also on the radio she comes through
von Kopf bis Fuß auf Liebe eingestellt, from head to toe
attuned to love

Briefly earth tears -
Berlin Dreißiger Jahre, Berlin in the thirties

und überall, and everywhere
Wege zum Glück - roads to happiness

Revisited the house, the tree felled
the polder almost filled

the road is straight, my life off track
so far, I still glance back

Flight information

A stewardess plays emergency theatre
the evening star drifts into the window
the moon lies on its back

time is finally stopped
we hang in the air
Till beneath, red brown, land shows up

trembling on its foundations
sucking us in like a magnet
a dust cloud rolls over a path of sand

The shadow of the plane
races towards a minaret
a flat and the light

restlessness that creeps up
when something touches the ground
of things

Family council at the river

Under the noon heat remain seated
under an age thick chestnut
at the café *The Ferry* where a narrow
Meuse brings cooling down

the slide wears a child's dress, the swing
refuses decay, and we, family,
reunited briefly talk up a storm
about the brevity of life

Later it would become quieter, avoided
less by the chickens, seeing in the distance
how the tow barge brought over bikers
and the sun stretching itself over the water

This wasn't our world
this were we

Snow

Snow is a fairy tale
a virginal whore

with her immaculate appearance
she is the queen of surface

But she cheats you from her depths
when at noon murmuring

she burns up and through her skin
again questions shimmer

Homecoming

Wholeheartedly lived against death
till something unexpected mirrors you
for instance in a poem, so

fragile that you never thought
that it existed
That wrings itself

through all your pores, rises
from the paper and
looks at you like a doe

That is a homecoming:
to see who you are
in this moment

The art of writing poetry

I believe in the dandelion plume
which is quite a strain to catch

and that in one sigh you can blow away
as soon as you're bored

That leaves one so much room
it almost isn't there when it is

but that with delicate barbs
still binds the earth to itself

Islands

THE boat to Ameland is empty
the waves break against the rail
ashtrays tinkle to the tune of the engines

we sit forlorn within ourselves, see
the quay nearing, how lamps sway
and old rain drifts over houses

Now the wind ambushes every thought
a harmonica murmurs
that the girl is pretty

and the lonesome laugh
of a woman to a man
pulses through the parlour

Schiermonnikoog

Here now the light doesn't shimmer
the chairs on the beachside café
squat together like veterans

so it happened between us
and everything from days gone by is silver:
this island, the sea, the birds

Passing ships have come and gone
Just you and me to lean upon
But the seagulls screamed it was time

What remains is a blurred picture
your henna hair windblown at a sea
this charming-winning liar

Opmerkingen, Bemerkungen, Remarks

Brockenspektrum: Ein optisches Phänomen, das auch Brockengespenst genannt wird, das auf dem höchsten Berg im Harz erscheint. Lichterscheinung bei Nebelwetterlage.

*

Brocken spectre: Optisch verschijnsel, genoemd naar de Brocken, de top van het Harzgebergte: een schaduw in de mist, voorzien van een aureool, wordt driedimensionaal afgebeeld als een schijnbaar gigantische figuur.

*

Brocken spectre: Optical phenomenon named after the Brocken Mountain, the highest peak in the Harz Mountains: a shadow in the mist, enhanced with a halo, is reflected in three dimensions as a seemingly gigantic figure.

Übersetzung Deutsch:
Fred Schywek
Translation English:
Annmarie Sauer
Except (What night does to a harbour; The woman who lives within me; The art of writing poetry)
translated by **Willem Groenewegen**

BIO

Job Degenaar (* Dubbeldam, NL 1952)
Dichter und Sänger
JD ist Präsident des niederländischen Zweiges des PEN-Writers-in-Prison-Komitees, das sich um gefangene Schreiber/innen in der Welt kümmert. Der Charakter seiner Gedichte ist melancholisch, zuweilen politisch-sozial und immer gefärbt durch Lebensweisheit, die auch auf Reisen, wie etwa nach Japan, gewachsen und verfeinert ist. Er lebt in Friesland, der Provinz, die schon immer durch großes Selbstständigkeitsbewußtsein in den Niederlanden hervorsticht, kennt die Sorge der Ausländer hier im Polderland.

Job Degenaar (* Dubbeldam, Nederland, 1952)
dichter en zanger
Tussen 1976 tot 2012 verschenen van hem een dozijn bundels. Zijn poëzie is doorvoeld en op onnadrukkelijke wijze geëngageerd. Deze betrokkenheid bij de wereld zet hij in de praktijk om door zijn voorzitterschap van het Writers in Prison Committee van PEN Nederland. De levenswijsheid die in Jobs gedichten naar melancholie neigt, brengt vertroosting voor de lezer. De gedichten zijn toegankelijk, verruimen de blik op de wereld dank zij de diepere waarneming van de reiziger en de zorgvuldige formulering van de dichter.

*

Job Degenaar (* Dubbeldam, The Netherlands, 1952)
poet and singer

Between 1976 and 2012 a dozen volumes of poetry by Degenaar has been published. His poetry is deeply felt and not explicitly committed. This commitment is however put in practice by his presidency of the Writers in Prison Committee for PEN The Netherlands. His broad outlook upon life veers in Job's poetry towards melancholy, yet his work offers consolation to the reader. The poems are inviting, open one's eyes to the wider world thanks to the fine observations of the traveller and the precise formulation of the poet.

*

BIBLIO

Bericht voor gelovigen, De Beuk, Amsterdam 1976 (s.d.) - **Het wak**, U.M. Holland, Haarlem 1980 - **'t Vlak ligt klaar**, Opwenteling, Eindhoven 1989 - **Linia przypływu (Vloedlijn)**, een bloemlezing van zijn poëzie bij de University of Wroclaw Press, 1991 Wroclaw (Polen), in het Pools vertaald door dr. **Jerzy Koch** - **De helderheid van morgens**, Thomas Rap, Amsterdam 1992 - **Van de arena en het lastdier**, Thomas Rap, Amsterdam 1995 - **Dus dit is zomer**, Thomas Rap, Amsterdam 1998 - **Huisbroei**, Thomas Rap (De Bezige Bij), Amsterdam 2003 - **Handkussen van de tijd**, een bloemlezing uit de eerste zeven bundels, Liverse, Dordrecht 2009, tweede druk 2010, derde uitgebreide druk 2012 - **Een onschuldige dag**, gedicht met inkjetprent van **Gerrit Westerveld** (bibliofiele uitgave, genummerde oplage), uitgeverij Kleinood & Grootzeer 2011- **Vluchtgegevens** Liverse, Dordrecht 2011 (met cd).

*

world internet books

wib.panorama - poetry for the world
Anthology - Anthologie - Bloemlezing

*

Grenzland
Werkbuch - Werkboek

*

Flußschiffahrt
Inland Waterways - Binnenvaart
Anthologie zur Kulturhauptstadt Europas Ruhrgebiet 2010
Cultural Capital of Europe 2010

*

ANTI
Anti-War Anthology - Antikriegsanthologie
Antioorlog Bloemlezing

*

Hafenklänge - Havenklanken
Sounds of Harbour
Sons du Port

*

Die Liebe in Holland und Flandern
De Liefde in Holland en Vlaanderen
Love in Holland and Flanders

*

Global Night Car
Weltnachtauto - Wereldnacht auto
Experimental work book

world internet books

Job Degenaar
Ich bin - I am

*

Paul Gellings
Stem van de herfst - Stimme des Herbstes

*

Roger Nupie
Lighthouse - Lichthaus - Lighthouse

*

Annie Reniers
Letters of Light - Buchstabenlicht -
Letters van Licht

*

Fred Schywek
Felsenleiter - Rockstairs
Weiße Mühle - Witte molen - White mill

*

Annmarie Sauer
Traces - Spuren - Sporen

*

Lucienne Stassaert
In one breath - In één adem - In einem Atemzug

*

Bart Stouten
Offenes Herz - Open hart - Open heart

*

world internet books
Duisburg/Rhein - Antwerpen - Hamburg

Herstellung und Verlag:
Books on Demand GmbH, Norderstedt
ISBN 978-3-8423-2862-4